A Color & Learn Guide

How to Care for Your
DOG

Janet Skiles

DOVER PUBLICATIONS, INC.
Mineola, New York

Dogs are great companions! They are fun to play with and make great pets, but they do need care and attention from you to remain happy and healthy. In this coloring book are tips on how to keep your dog safe, what to do when you bring a new puppy home, how to "puppy proof" your home, and more. You can color the pages with crayons, pencils, or markers. There is also a chart on page 30 to keep track of your daily dog care.

Bibliographical Note

How to Care for Your Dog: A Color & Learn Guide for Kids is a new work,
first published by Dover Publications, Inc., in 2011.

International Standard Book Number

ISBN-13: 978-0-486-48149-4
ISBN-10: 0-486-48149-2

Manufactured in the United States by LSC Communications
48149205   2017
www.doverpublications.com

You can adopt a puppy or dog from a local animal shelter or a pet shop. Be sure to choose the best match for your lifestyle. Puppies are very active and need training and a lot of exercise. Older dogs can be more laid back and are sometimes already trained.

You will need to "puppy proof" your home by getting down on the floor so you can see things at their level. Pick up anything that looks like a choking hazard such as paper clips, plastic bags, rubber bands, ribbons, and Christmas tree tinsel.

Puppies like to chew things, so keep phone cords and electric wires hidden or out of reach. Also, check to make sure the plants in your home are not poisonous. If they are, or you are not sure, give them away to friends who don't have pets.

3

A new companion will need to visit the veterinarian (pet doctor) for vaccinations and a check-up. The veterinarian will tell you everything you need to know about keeping your pet healthy.

When you first bring your new puppy home he might be scared
and cry a little at night. This is because it might be the first
time he is away from the pack (dog family). To stop this, put the
crate or kennel next to your bed so he is not alone.

Make sure you feed your companion the correct dog food for his
age and weight. Dogs go through different stages in life and their
diet needs to be adjusted as they grow. Resist giving your dog
table scraps, as this can cause him to become overweight.

Your dog should have fresh, clean water available to drink throughout the day. They especially need water on a hot day, after playing, and with a meal. So keep your eyes out to see if the water bowl needs to be refilled!

Always have your puppy wear a collar with an identification tag attached to it. The tag should have your address and phone number on it. This way, if your dog ever gets lost whoever finds her will be able to contact you.

To keep your dog's coat shiny and healthy, he will need regular brushing. Ask your veterinarian which is the best type of brush to use for your dog. Use gentle strokes and give him a few treats after you are done.

After you are done brushing your dog, he will be ready for a bath. You will need towels and special shampoo made just for dogs. First get him wet, apply the shampoo, and rinse. Be careful not to get it in his eyes and ears!

There's nothing a dog likes more than playing outside in the
fresh air! Running, fetching, and catching a flying disk are just
some of the many fun activities that you can do with your dog.
They are not only fun; they are great exercise!

When your dog is outside, make sure she has shelter from the
rain and sun and has plenty of water. Your yard should be clean,
fenced, and free of poisonous plants.
Don't ever leave your dog outside unsupervised.

Many dogs are scared of thunder and lightning storms and will become very nervous. Closing the windows and curtains and turning up the television or radio will help block the noise. If you stay calm, your dog will stay calm!

Dogs love to go for walks! You can walk her by attaching a leash
to her collar, or a harness. Make sure that the collar fits her
correctly. You should only be able to fit two fingers between her
neck and the collar, otherwise she could slip out of it.

Dogs like people, but also need to be friends with other dogs.
Socialize your dog by introducing him to new people and
other dogs. See if there are any other nice puppies in your
neighborhood available for a play date with your pup.

Dogs can sometimes get hurt while they are playing. If your dog
gets hurt, bring him to the veterinarian as soon as possible.
The vet will examine him and tell you what you have to do
so your dog can start feeling better.

16

Sometimes puppies can get confused and chew things they
aren't supposed to chew—like a shoe. If this happens to you,
don't grab the shoe out of her mouth, get one of her dog toys
and offer it to trade it with her for the shoe.

17

Puppies need to be carefully watched while indoors until they are housebroken. If you see that your dog is sniffing around, whimpering, or circling, you should make a startling noise and bring her right outside on her leash. Preventing an accident is the best cure!

18

When you get outside with your puppy, bring him over to the same "potty" spot each time. Stand there until he starts going, then say "potty." The second he finishes going give him a treat and plenty of praise.

When you can't watch your puppy, temporarily put her in a crate
big enough to stand, lie down, and turn around in.
A crate is similar to a den and will make her feel secure.
Most dogs will not have accidents in the crate.

Sit: Take a treat in your hand, hold it up to your dog's nose, then move your hand up, over, and past his head and he will automatically sit. Right before he sits, say "sit." When he sits give him a treat right away and praise him.

Down: Take a treat in your hand, hold it up to your dog's nose,
then move your hand slowly down and place your hand between
her feet. When she starts to move down say "down."
When she is down give her a treat right away and praise her.

Always be safe when meeting new dogs. Don't assume all dogs
are friendly. First ask the owner if you can pet their dog.
If the owner says yes, let the dog sniff the back of your hand,
then pet him under the chin.

If you are approached by a strange dog stay calm and stand still.
Do not scream or run away! Speak softly to the dog and don't
make eye contact. A friendly dog will look happy with a wagging
tail. An unfriendly dog will bark, growl, or show teeth.

If a dog knocks you down, lie on your stomach and protect your head and ears with your arms. Try to stay calm until help arrives. The dog will probably leave you alone if you remain still.

Dogs need to be alone sometimes, just like humans!
Some dogs get very upset when they are bothered while chewing
a bone, eating dinner, or having a drink. Also, when he is in his
resting place, do not disturb him.

Give your companion plenty of love and he will give it right back to you! If you provide daily exercise, playtime, fresh food and water, and veterinary care, you will have a happy, healthy best friend for years to come.

Daily Dog Care	Monday	Tuesday	Wednesday	Thursday	Friday	Saturday	Sunday
Love and praise dog							
Feed dog							
Give dog water							
Take your dog for a walk							
Play with dog							
Brush dog							
Make sure dangerous objects are out of dog's reach							
More love, petting and praise							